WOOLTON & GATEACRE

Architecture and Heritage

© A Moscardini 2008

Published by The Bluecoat Press, Liverpool.
Book design by MARCH Graphic Design Studio, Liverpool.
Printed by Grafo.

ISBN 1 904438 43 1

Front cover. Church Road. All the buildings seen in this
sketch are listed for their architectural and historic interest.
Back cover. The entrance to Woolton Mount.

Tony Moscardini studied at the Glasgow School of Art, the Glasgow
School of Architecture and Strathclyde University. He has worked in
private practice, local government, the New Towns and the Planning
Inspectorate. He has lived in Woolton for many years and hopes this
book will qualify him as a 'Wooltonian'.

WOOLTON & GATEACRE

Architecture and Heritage

Anthony Moscardini

The Bluecoat Press

Contents

Much Woolton's **Village Cross** is thought to be at least 400 years old and has amazingly survived virtual demolition and at least three removals before settling on the site outside the former Corporation office. Its continuing existence can be attributed to Alderman Mather of Beechwood who restored it to its present state, on its present site, to commemorate the end of Woolton's life as a self-governing community in 1913 when it was absorbed into Liverpool.

Listing does not apply only to buildings. The **Boundary Stones** between Much Woolton and Little Woolton (the Meer Stones) can be found at the corner of Church Road and Reservoir Road. They are Grade II listed and date back to 1658, when Woolton's boundaries were first determined.

No. 30 Allerton Road, now Moorcroft's Solicitors, marks a busy intersection in the centre of the village.

Introduction

The village of Woolton dates from Anglo-Saxon times and appeared in the *Domesday Book* in 1086, where it was recorded as *Ulventune or Little Woolton*. No part of the original village remains and it was not until the Industrial Revolution, in the late nineteenth century, that Woolton Village grew into the sizeable settlement that we now know. This growth took two distinct forms: the large Italianate villas, set in spacious grounds, on the higher ground of Woolton Mount and Church Road to the north, and the terraced artisans' and tradesmen's dwellings clustered around Allerton Road. Although these areas differ widely in character, there is a visual unity, achieved through the vertical scale and proportion of the buildings and the use of local sandstone, red brick and dark slate.

In spite of the banal design quality and unsympathetic scale of more recent infill development, as well as the ill-judged replacement of original features, such as doors and windows on both houses and shops, the village still retains its character, and local community groups maintain constant pressure for high standards in the face of an indifferent local authority. The focus of the village is Lodes Pond which has been extended and improved in recent years almost entirely through the efforts of these groups and local councillors, who persuaded the Highway Authority to spend the monies made available by the supermarket developers, on improvements for pedestrians and amenity, rather than on spurious roadworks that would have destroyed the character of the village centre.

Woolton Village is now a Conservation Area and an award-winning 'Village in Bloom'. It contains over 150 buildings regarded as being of 'Architectural or Historic Merit', ranging from a humble boundary stone, to Woolton Hall, one of the country's relatively few Grade I listed buildings. This sketchbook seeks to commemorate these buildings and, more importantly, bring them to the attention of the public at large.

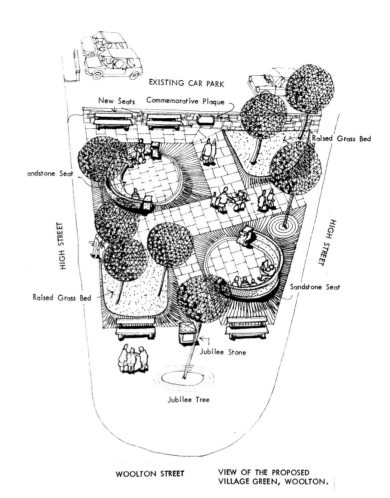

EXISTING CAR PARK — New Seats — Commemorative Plaque — Raised Grass Bed — andstone Seat — HIGH STREET — HIGH STREET — Raised Grass Bed — Sandstone Seat — Jubilee Stone — Jubilee Tree

WOOLTON STREET   VIEW OF THE PROPOSED
VILLAGE GREEN, WOOLTON.

Design drawing for the laying out of the derelict land at Woolton Street / High Street as the Commemorative Jubilee Garden. The layout used salvaged granite setts and york paving with, as a feature, circular sandstone seats saved from the demolition contractors when Druids Cross House disappeared to make way for a block of flats. The adjoining car park occupies the site of the former Woolton Tram terminus.

The Jubilee Garden makes an ideal starting point for walks around Woolton's buildings

Around the Village Centre

The village centre contains a variety of building styles and uses. The banks, in particular, reflect the corporate identity that used to be projected through a house style, rather than as it is today, through media advertising.

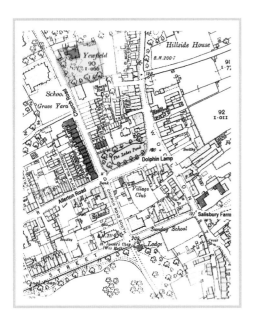

Listing need not only apply to buildings – the late nineteenth century **Dolphin Lamp** which marks the centre is Grade II listed and is similar to those fronting St George's Hall in the city centre.

The **Woolton Cinema** has become part of the fabric of the village and there is no doubt that community life would be diminished if it were to disappear. Design work for the cinema was started by its architect, L.G. Pritchard ARIBA, in 1925, and construction work followed shortly afterwards at an estimated cost of £10,000.

A magistrate's licence was granted in 1927. To make full use of the small site, the auditorium was set at an angle to Mason Street. Steps lead to the small foyer, which in turn gives access to the rear of the stadium-type auditorium. Originally, it had 800 seats but these were reduced in 1930 to 600, when the screen was moved forward to house the speaker that was required on the introduction of sound movies. Today, discounting the new 'multiplexes', it is one of only three survivors of the district's 118 cinemas. During its 70-year life it has been closed only twice, once for three months when it was

almost completely destroyed by fire. It was then virtually rebuilt and modernised with cinemascope and more generously spaced seating to accommodate an audience of 612, reopening in December 1958. The latest renovation was in 1984 when, together with air-conditioning, the seating was reduced to 250 comfortable armchairs.

More recently, on the death of its owner, the building was in danger of falling into the hands of developers, but was fortunately saved by the sterling efforts of a group of community-minded cinema enthusiasts.

The building was suggested for listing at the last review but this was declined by English Heritage, probably because of the unsympathetic canopy design and the superfluous white 'styling' panels that obscure the façade.

No. 8 Church Road forms the return to the stone-built terrace facing Lodes Pond. Dating from the early nineteenth century, it is Grade II listed.

No. 1 Mason Street is a late Georgian house with a stone base, the remaining three storeys being of hand-made brick with stone quoins. The main building is of an unusual single aspect design.

The Elephant Hotel (Grade II listed) situated at the end of Woolton Street, was once a private house. The date stone, 1772, is not accurate, as the present building dates from the early nineteenth century with later additions. The carved elephant's head leaves no doubt as to the building's name, and together with the iron balconies, makes an attractive feature of the public house. The original inn sign (also listed) still survives.

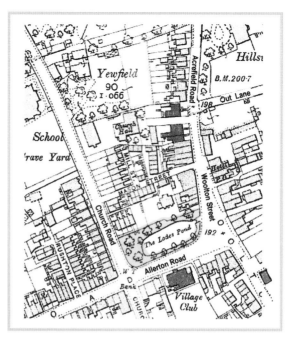

No. 15 Church Road. Part of the early nineteenth century Grade II listed terrace which stretches from No. 7 to No. 35 Church Road. Brick built, with sandstone trim, a number of the houses have ornate latticed porches.

The **Coffee House** on Woolton Street has a date stone showing 1641, although this was probably reset from the original building on the site. Although much altered, it is surely the oldest public house in the village and was conveniently situated to serve passengers travelling to and from the city centre by coach and horse during late nineteenth century.

Woolton House, the rear of St Peter's Hall, Greenbank and the White Horse public house.

Woolton House, Nos. 4 and 6 Woolton Street, are made up from two late nineteenth century town houses of decorated brick with stone quoins and window/door trim.

The houses have always been connected with medical practice and before conversion to its present use, as the Woolton House Medical Centre, it was the residence of Doctor Carl Warner MC, a prominent figure in Woolton folklore. As a young doctor he carried out his visits using a pony and trap. These were, no doubt, housed in the stable block to the rear. Both the houses and stable are Grade II listed.

The **Village Club**, built in 1885, provides social facilities for all Woolton residents and continues to be at the centre of village life.

Greenbank, No. 2
Woolton Street, is an
early nineteenth century
brick-built house with
original windows. It is
Grade II listed. The
porch is a later addition.

Former public convenience and shelter, Lodes
Pond, once served the needs of villagers in the
shopping centre. The rear included covered seating
overlooking Lodes Pond when it was a pleasant
amenity, rather than the present car park. The
building was saved from dereliction by conversion
into its present Estate Agency use.

CHURCH ROAD WOOLTON

Church Road. Woolton's listed road. All the buildings seen in
this sketch are listed for their architectural and historic interest.
It is the best example of buildings in the village, which have
been kept true to their original design by good maintenance and
sympathetic restoration. The significance of **St Peter's Church**
as a landmark building can be appreciated.

16

Shop, No. 30 Allerton Road, listed Grade II. The only listed shop premises in the village, it has survived with its original features intact, unlike the remainder of the shopping area, where the original façades have been hacked away to make way for unsightly shutters and plastic canopies. Dating back to the early nineteenth century, it is of brick with stone dressings. Of note are the two stone panels on the first floor inscribed Allerton Road and Church Road.

The shop started life as a grocer's, then later became an optician's, before its present use as a solicitor's office.

Lake House, No. 27 Allerton Road, built of brick with stone dressings, is now only a façade, with the interior forming part of the adjoining bank. Lake House is early nineteenth century Grade II listed.

Around the Baths

Door detail at **61a Allerton Road.**

No. 61 and 61a Allerton Road are part of a nineteenth century stone building with a slate roof and blank windows on the side. Originally a public house, the building has had a number of uses in its lifetime. The present owner, whilst retaining part of the premises as a gentleman's hairdresser, has sympathetically converted the remainder to residential use. The front courtyard is laid out in granite paving, which contributes to the attractive setting of the building. It is Grade II listed and is a notable landmark in this part of the village.

No. 90 Allerton Road, next to the library, is a typical late nineteenth century, two-storey terrace house.

One of a number of terracotta sculptured plaques built into the brickwork of the Baths.

Although not listed, **Woolton Baths** is a building of note in this part of the village. Built in the late nineteenth century by the then Urban District Council, it embodies the standards of quality which used to be the norm for public buildings and is representative of the era. Frequently threatened with closure, it nevertheless survives, together with the library, as one of Woolton's last public buildings.

Woolton's Churches
St Mary's and its environs

Woolton's unique character derives from its churches and church buildings. Their use of the area's topography, combined with sandstone from the local quarry, confirms their status as landmark buildings in the village.

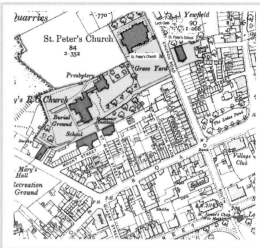

Location Plan 1904.

The St Mary's buildings from the library.

St Mary's Church from St Mary Street.

The **St Mary's Church buildings** are a remarkable example of their type. The present church was opened in 1860 and was known, until 1891, as St Bennet's, as was the chapel in Watergate Lane that it replaced. The church building cost £3,543, including £548 for the land. A Miss Simpson gave £1000 (the equivalent of £750,000 today); the Roskill family gave £500 and other private donations amounted to £500. A Miss Sarah Hampson paid off the balance and, in 1865, the Roskills donated the high altar, at a cost of £315. Built of Woolton sandstone, the church was designed by R.W. Hughes of Preston and is Grade II listed.

The distinguished architect Edward Pugin designed the later **Presbytery** (1864) and is also thought to be responsible for the reredos in the interior of the main church. His building uses similar materials to the church, to which it is connected by a corridor, thus emphasising its group value.

Mechanic's Institutes were first established in 1823 by the Unitarians for the education of the poor. The **Woolton Institute** building dates from 1849 and contained the only public library in the village at that time. It enjoyed only partial success and by the end of the century it was put to other uses, one of which was as a dancing academy. Its last public use was as a dining room for the adjoining St Mary's school. It now enjoys a new lease of life as a superbly converted private dwelling, setting a standard for rehabilitation that, unfortunately, is only rarely seen in the conservation area.

The former Mechanics Institute, St Mary Street.

Former Parish Hall, St Mary's Church, Parish Centre and Mount Street.
The former St Mary's Hall and the St Mary's group of buildings as seen from Quarry Street.

Although, not part of this group, the nearby **Woolton Wesleyan Methodist Chapel** is a building of merit. This Grade II listed building started life in 1834 as the Wesleyan Methodist Chapel, serving their congregation for more than 30 years. It was then used as a school until its present use as Woolton Library. As a chapel it was entered from the street by a centrally placed arched door and steps. This was still a feature of the building until 1924, when it was replaced by the present side door and was converted to library use.

St Mary's Parish Centre, formerly the Much Woolton RC School, seen here from Mount Street, dates back to the 1860s and is built of local stone with a slate roof. With its bridge entry, it is a good example of how a building can solve the transition between different ground levels and rock outcrops. This, and the previous buildings, form part of a group of Grade II listed buildings. Mention should be made of the adjoining **Necropolis** and the former **St Mary's Hall** (originally Reynolds Hall) now a dwelling house, in Quarry Street, all of which contribute towards this memorable group.

St Peter's Church and its environs

The attractive churchyard is entered by way of a half-timbered **Lych Gate** that is also listed Grade II.

The present **St Peter's Anglican Church** replaced an earlier chapel on the site. The present building dates back to 1887 and was designed by Grayson and Auld, Architects. The strong squat tower is an imposing landmark that can be seen for many miles around. It is a building of national significance, being graded II*, a category that includes only 45 per cent of the country's listed buildings.

St Peter's Parish Rooms, opposite
the church, are also listed Grade II.

The former **United Reform Church** at the corner of High Street
and Quarry Street South, was built in 1865, initially as the
Congregational Church. The building was impressive in those days
and, although no longer used as a church, it remains a landmark
building in the centre of the village. The architects, W and J Hay
of Liverpool, have been ingenious in the use of decorative stone
and subtle geometrical shapes, most notably in the main circular
window and prominent spire. It is now used as a residential home
and the style of the alterations required to accommodate this use,
is probably the reason why it is not listed.

Around Woolton Hall

Woolton Hall is one of nine buildings in Liverpool listed as Grade I. These are considered to be of 'outstanding interest', and Woolton is indeed fortunate to have one such in the village. The present building, of sandstone ashlar, dates back to 1704 and was the home of Richard Molyneux, whose family lived on the site for many years. The Hall was purchased in 1772 by Nicholas Ashton, a Liverpool gentleman with interests in canals, salt and shipping, who in 1774 commissioned Robert Adam to remodel its interior and exterior. The façade is still much as Adam designed it, apart from the massive porte cochère, at the front, and the single-storey apse to the new dining room, at the rear. The four medallions at the front depict classical scenes. In early 1900 the house was owned by the McGuffie family and was used as a hydropathic establishment known as the Hydro. Following wartime use, the house and grounds came into the ownership of the Notre Dame religious order, who established a High School on the site, using the hall for teaching purposes.

When, in 1973, the school expanded into the present St Julie's High School building, the hall was declared redundant and was said to be incapable of other use by its owners, who sought permission to demolish it. The Planning Authority and the general public vigorously resisted this, and, the Woolton Society was established at that date, 30 years ago, in order to coordinate local opposition to the proposal. A comprehensive survey report carried out by local Architect and Historian, Janet Gnosspelius, and commissioned by the City Planning Department, proved, contrary to the evidence provided by the applicants, that the building was in a relatively good state of repair and capable of economical use. The Hall was subsequently refurbished and was used for function rooms until recently.

Woodleigh, former lodge to Woolton Hall.

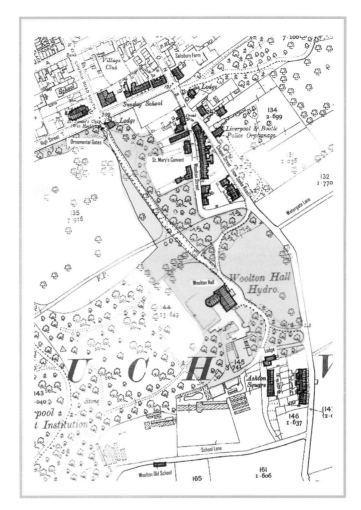

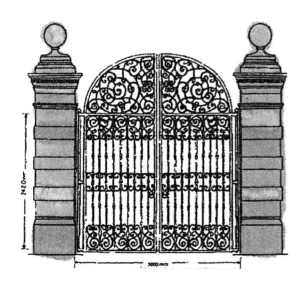

Ornamental gates, former gateway to Woolton Hall.

Listed Buildings associated with Woolton Hall

Woolton Hall was very much part of the village in 1904. Another listed building, associated with the Hall, is **Woodleigh**, in the central reservation of High Street. The former lodge is built of red sandstone in the classical style with Greek Doric columns and sculptured ornamental frieze. It is Grade II listed.

The **Ornamental Gates**, also Grade II listed, are today merely an exact replica of the originals which, after years of neglect, were accidentally demolished by the Council. The Woolton Society was responsible for insisting that listed statutory procedures were followed, ensuring that they were reinstated. Both the lodge and the gates contain details and materials that have an affinity with the Hall. It is not difficult, even now, to visualise the route of the main carriageway approach to the Hall.

A number of listed buildings adjoin Woolton Hall and owe their origin to the Hall, serving it in various ways. Entered by a cul-de-sac from School Lane is **Ashton Square**, a terrace of cottages built for the estate workers of Woolton Hall and dating from the late eighteenth century.

Built of brick, with local sandstone used for the Gothic arches over the doors and windows, the majority of this group remains in nearly its original form, although the end terrace house has been inexplicably cement rendered, obliterating the original brickwork. Much of the original cobbled footpath survives intact and the whole group is Grade II listed.

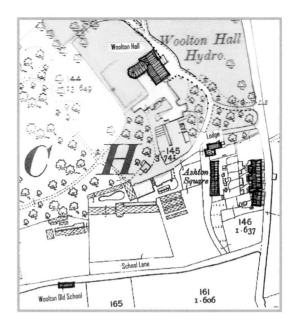

View of Ashton Square.

No. 5 Ashton square.

Woolton Old School, School Lane, is the oldest building in Woolton, dating back to the early seventeenth century (the date 1610 inscribed over the doorway is thought to have been carved in more recent years and is not historically accurate). The unusually large blocks of stone used in its construction, as well the Gothic windows, give rise to speculation that the building is of an earlier date and, indeed, it is possibly the earliest elementary school in Lancashire.

Bearing in mind that for many years whilst in Council ownership, the building was left open to the elements, as a store for the Parks Department, it is a tribute to its construction and hardy materials that it has survived to the present day. Like many neglected listed buildings, it was saved when it was sold for conversion to a private residence. Following this use, it has been restored to a semblance of its original purpose, as a children's day nursery. It is Grade II listed.

Woolton Hall Lodge is located on the Speke Road entrance to the Hall. Grade II listed, it is dated nineteenth century, and is built in sandstone with a slated roof.

Around Woolton Street

The Woolton Street area as it was in 1904. The west side of Woolton Street once contained both **St Mary's Convent** and **Dicky Ball's Cottage**; a **seventeenth century terrace** built in local stone; a **town house** built in dressed stone with a projecting classical porch and columns; and the original **Brown's Newsagents,** subsequently relocated to its present premises.

Woolton Street as it is today. The red brick terrace comprising nos. 33 to 47, dates back to the nineteenth century, and is one of the least unspoilt terraces in the village.

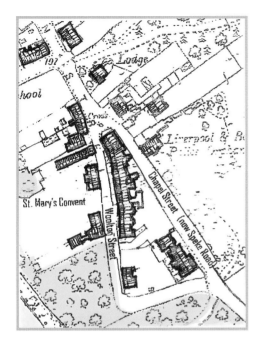

A sketch showing Woolton Street before the Council's housing steamroller razed many of the buildings to the ground, replacing them with the present flats. These are standard municipal housing designs of their era with no concession made to their location, other than some token panels of sandstone. It is ironic to think that had the original buildings survived to the present day, they would have been snapped up for rehabilitation and sold at astronomical prices!

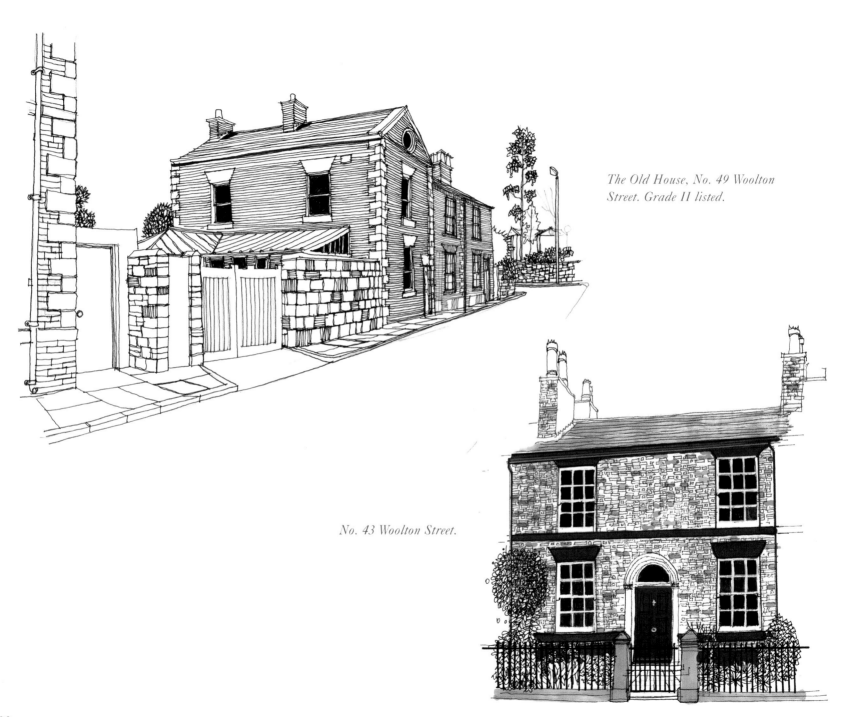

The Old House, No. 49 Woolton Street. Grade II listed.

No. 43 Woolton Street.

The **Former Corporation Offices** at No. 33 Woolton Street, now converted into a house, date back to the time before the village was absorbed into the City of Liverpool. Of brick construction, trimmed with sandstone, it is a prominent landmark in this part of the village. Grade II listed, it has survived unaltered and is in excellent condition.

Around High Street

The **Salisbury Farm** buildings date back to the seventeenth century. For over 300 years the dairy was a focal point in the life of the village. The house and shop, together with the cobbled courtyard and the old farm buildings, form an interesting group and are Grade II listed. A landscape contractor now uses the site as a depot.

Nos. 14 and 16 High Street. High Street comprises a number of semi-detached and terraced houses, of which these are the most prominent with their white rendered finish. They are Grade II listed.

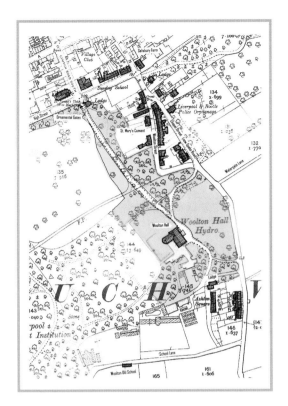

No. 22 High Street retains its original windows and is a good example of a three storey late nineteenth century town house. Much visual damage has been caused to historic housing by ill-judged window replacement. Fortunately the Grade II listed terrace, **Nos. 20 to 32**, is predominantly in its original form. It features decorative brick construction, sandstone quoins and mouldings and natural slate roofs.

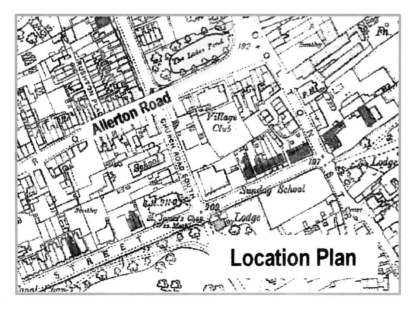

Location Plan

No. 36 Woolton Street and Nos. 2a to 12 High
Street form a group of Grade II listed late
nineteenth century houses occupying a prime
position in the village centre. Built in various
shades of patterned brick, with sandstone trim and
slate roofs, they are particularly notable for their
sensitive retention of original architectural
features and the evident high standard of care and
maintenance – they set an example to be followed
elsewhere in the conservation area.

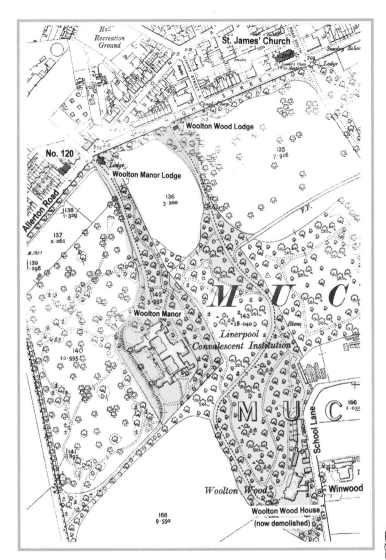

Location Plan as in 1904.

Woolton Wood Lodge is a brick built
Victorian building with stone Dutch gables.

Woolton Manor Lodge (or Heaton Lodge)
unlike the other lodges, is a substantial two-
storey building. The rusticated stonework
reflects the solid style of its parent house,
Woolton Manor.

St James' Church dates from 1886. Built of local red sandstone, it is in the Decorated Gothic style. Although not listed, the church has an unusual highly moulded corner tower and forms a group with an equally attractive church hall opposite.

No. 120 Allerton Road is an early Grade II listed nineteenth century Regency house, now divided into two dwellings. Stucco with a hipped slate roof, the replacement windows imitate the original sashes. At the front is a Gothic timber and glass porch, flanked by shallow bay windows with cornices and parapets.

*Public Convenience and
Shelter, High Street, Woolton.*

Liverpool owes its present-day form to two inspired Chief Officers, City Engineer James Brodie and City Architect Lancelot Keay who, between the wars, did brilliant work in developing the outer areas of the city. The landscaped dual carriageways, with a central reservation for public transport, led the way in highway design. Kings Drive was to be part of the Outer Ring Road but, with the post-war lack of confidence in the city, was never completed, leaving a legacy of congested village centres.

Lancelot Keay spent 23 years in the service of the city and was responsible for the 'Garden City'-type suburbs developed around the framework of Brodie's roads. Neo-Georgian in style, carefully detailed and well proportioned, they are among the best housing examples of the era. The Hunts Cross Avenue estate, nominally a conservation area, was a good example of his work but is now so altered in appearance that the original design cohesion is all but lost.

Keay was also responsible for stylish public buildings of all sizes. The **Former Public Convenience and Shelter** on High Street served the village and tram terminus in its heyday but sadly now lies closed and neglected. The Council appears to have neither the wit to find another use for it, nor the inclination to dispose of it to someone who can!

Church Road – Listed Houses

In the nineteenth century, Woolton's wooded slopes proved an attractive setting for successful Liverpool merchants to build their houses. Many grand houses were built during that era and they remain today as Grade II listed buildings. James Rose, a self-made man of that time, known as the 'King of Woolton', opened Woolton Quarry and built many houses, from humble cottages in Rose Street and Rose Brow, to the grandeur of **Beechwood** – which he built for his own use – and **Rosemount**, later the Archbishop's House, both on Church Road. Both are built in the same style with matching features.

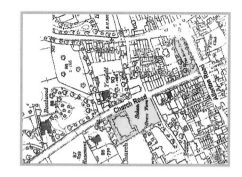

Beechwood, Church Road. Early nineteenth century. Sandstone with slate roof. Doric colonnaded entrance with ornamental cornice.

Yewfield, Church Road. Early nineteenth century stucco with slate roof. Now hidden from the road since its grounds were redeveloped with new housing, but it is still prominent on the skyline when viewed from Woolton Woods. In 1904 it was occupied by Arthur Stanley Mather, Solicitor.

No. 29 Church Road. One of a terrace of mid-nineteenth century, brick built, middle-income houses, which is notable for its latticed timber porch. These houses were mainly occupied by tradesmen and shopkeepers. In 1904 this house was occupied by John Davies, described as a 'car proprietor'.

Rosemount, Church Road. Detail of main façade. Early nineteenth century, built of sandstone with distinctive incised pilasters and a central Doric porch. On conversion into flats, the roof has been much raised and dormer windows added to provide an additional floor of living accommodation.

Woolton's Listed Houses

Woolton's leafy setting proved attractive to nineteenth century Liverpool merchants and many large houses were built on the high ground adjoining the village. Many of these have survived, although rarely in the ownership of the original families, nor do they remain as single dwellings, or in their original use. Those that remain are Grade II listed and contribute greatly to the city's architectural heritage.

Knolle Park, dates from the late nineteenth century and is of painted ashlar with a slate roof. The dominant feature is a very fine portico of four classical columns supporting a decorated architrave. The ground floor windows are simply treated, whilst those in the upper floors have moulded surrounds. The building is now known as St Gabriel's Convent and is in use as a children's home.

This splendid Victorian villa on Glenrose Road is finished in stucco with stone quoins. The moulded cornice is supported on brackets and the centre portion has a porch with pilasters and a balustrade. The windows are in Venetian style with small leaded panels forming decorative patterns. The building is now divided into three separate dwellings **Strawberry House, Mossdene** and **Crawsfordsburn.**

Woolton Tower, Tower House and **Tower Cottage** form a distinctive group of late nineteenth century stone built buildings in Tower Way.

Beaconsfield House, Beaconsfield Road, is another Victorian villa built in red sandstone with twin pointed gables to the front and three to each side. Typical Gothic features are the labels over the stone-mullioned windows, the ogee arch over the door and the tall octagonal chimneys. It has now been restored to its former glory.

Woolton Mount's Listed Houses

The **Entrance to Woolton Mount.** The private roadway known as **Woolton Mount** gives access to a number of detached dwellings, the most notable of which are the three Grade II listed nineteenth century villas, **Bankside, The Mount** and **Acrefield House.** The roadway itself is of note, being uniquely paved with red sandstone slabs.

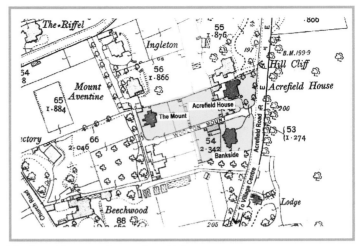

Woolton Mount as it was in 1904.

Bankside is a Victorian Gothic building with a castellated porch and elaborately carved barge boards. The stucco has been scored to resemble ashlar.

The Mount stands at the top of Woolton Mount and dates back to mid-nineteenth century. It is finished in stucco with a slate roof. All the houses have been kept in an excellent state of repair.

Acrefield House is a classical early Victorian villa in stucco with accentuated quoins. The porch is in the Greek Ionic style.

Woolton's Landmark Buildings

Built in 1911, the **Water Tower** in Reservoir Road marks the highest point in South Liverpool and is truly a landmark building. The reservoir has long since gone but this sturdy stone building remains as a symbol of an era when local authorities led by example, by commissioning high standards of design and quality of materials.

Of particular note is the classical entrance, **below,** to the side of the building. It is Grade II listed.

Many public houses were built in Woolton in the second half of nineteenth century. Not surprisingly, many of these were sited in Quarry Street, particularly around the quarry itself to serve the workers there. It is hardly a coincidence that the **Police Office** and **Court Room** were also located there!

Built in 1854, the **Village Inn is** built of sandstone with a slate roof. After a number of years it became the residence and studio of the sculptor Arthur Dooley, but it has now reverted to public house use.

The former **Police Office** and **Court Room** in Quarry Street set the standard for community policing and instant justice over a century ago. Although not listed, it is a landmark building in Woolton's history.

The **Victoria** is a good example of a Victorian pub. It has survived in its original state; unlike many of its contemporaries, it has avoided the tasteless 'modernising' carried out by the brewery companies in more recent years.

The Lodges of Woolton

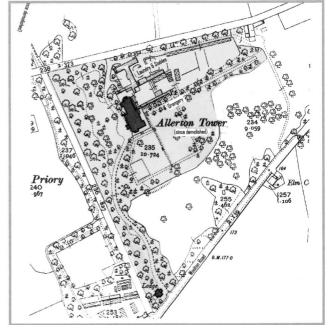

During the last century, many of Woolton's great houses have disappeared and their estates have either been ruined with largely unsympathetic development, taken up by roadworks or, with great foresight, absorbed into the village's unique public open space. The lodges, however, remain, and the quality of both their design and materials must have been replicated in the buildings they served and which have now been lost, either through neglect, or property speculation.

Harvey Lonsdale Elmes, architect for St George's Hall, designed all the buildings on the Allerton Tower estate. **The Lodge** is Grade II listed, as are the entrance gates. The estate itself is now a public open space and of the original buildings, apart from the lodge and gates, only the laundry and stable buildings remain. The only part of the main house which remains is the orangery.

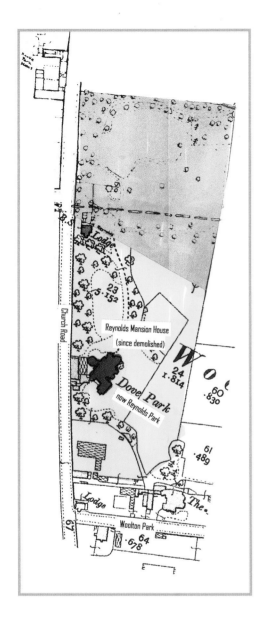

Riffel Lodge occupies a prominent position on the corner of Church Road and Woolton Park. It is built of brick and sandstone in the Tudor style with ornamental vertical tile finishes. It is dated 1859 and is Grade II listed. Riffel House survives, although the original grounds have long since been developed.

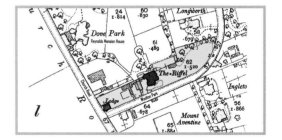

Reynolds Lodge, Church Road, is of brick with red tile roof and decorative tile hanging. The lower windows have stone mullions and a notable feature of the building is the open porch at the side with carved balusters. The original house, Dove Park no longer exists and the grounds are now part of Reynolds Park.

Amestry Court, Acrefield Road, with its **Lodge** and **Coachhouse** is a well-restored group of buildings. The main house is dated 1891 and is in red brick with a red tiled roof and tall ornamental chimneys. The Coachhouse, dated 1887, is also in red brick, with a projecting upper storey hung with red vertical tiles. The Lodge, 1884, is more ornate and is also built in matching red brick with a louvered cupola, topped by a weather vane. The prominent gable is clad partly by decorative tile hanging, with the remainder in black and white half timbering.

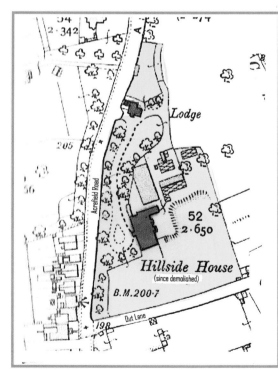

Camphill Lodge is the most ornate of all the lodges. Built of brick with sandstone trim and lavishly carved sandstone entrance porch and gable. It is a hidden gem in its now rather isolated position.

The lodge, **Blair Lea** is all that remains of the former Hillside House estate. Constructed of blue-banded brick with a slate roof, it dates from around 1870. Distinctive features are the turret, complete with gargoyle, and the short slate spire.

Gateacre (or Little Woolton)

Gateacre (also known as Little Woolton) was, until the 1950s, when it became an overspill area for post-war slum clearance in the city centre, a rural village of mixed character. It contains shops, houses, inns, a riding school and, until recently, manufacturing industry dating to the first quarter of the nineteenth century, when most of the buildings were built. These are mainly of red brick and sandstone with slated roofs and many of them are listed as buildings of architectural or historic interest. It is the smallest conservation area in the city but its distinctive black and white Tudor style buildings, centred on the village green, give it a unique and immediately recognisable identity.

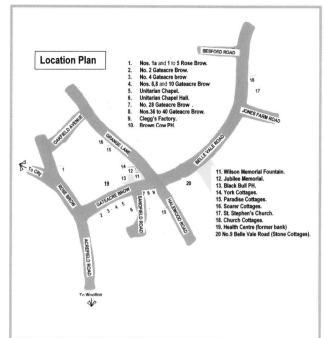

Location Plan

1. Nos. 1a and 1 to 5 Rose Brow.
2. No. 2 Gateacre Brow.
3. No. 4 Gateacre brow
4. Nos. 6,8 and 10 Gateacre Brow
5. Unitarian Chapel.
6. Unitarian Chapel Hall.
7. No. 28 Gateacre Brow .
8. Nos.36 to 40 Gateacre Brow.
9. Clegg's Factory.
10. Brown Cow PH.

11. Wilson Memorial Fountain.
12. Jubilee Memorial.
13. Black Bull PH.
14. York Cottages.
15. Paradise Cottages.
16. Soarer Cottages.
17. St. Stephen's Church.
18. Church Cottages.
19. Health Centre (former bank)
20 No.9 Belle Vale Road (Stone Cottages).

Approaching Gateacre village from Rose Brow, **Gateacre Brow** contains a number of small nineteenth century villas, each of distinctive design. **No. 2** is built of patterned brick with a slated roof, original sash windows and door fan light. Its excellent state of repair and respect for original features sets an example for listed properties of its era.

Nos. 1a and 1 to 5 Rose Brow form a small terrace of early nineteenth century brick cottages, with sandstone lintels and sills. The corner building of the group is of particular interest, with its carved sandstone window mullions and ornate door surround. The roof is of fish scale slates and the small dormers are topped with carved fleur-de-lis crested tiles. Recent times have seen the building used as a cobbler's, a corner shop (for which it seems ideal) and more recently, a nursery. The group is Grade II listed.

No. 4 Gateacre Brow is contemporary with its neighbour at No. 2, and is probably similar in plan and overall dimensions. It is built of sandstone, however, and has twelve-paned sash windows. This demonstrates that, unlike today, individual identity could be achieved without disrespect for neighbours and the urban design grain.

Nos. 6, 8 and **10 Gateacre Brow** form a small group with an added shop front. The houses are of sandstone ashlar, whilst the shop had an applied rendered finish which has now been removed to reveal a rough sandstone construction. They date from the mid-nineteenth century and the characteristic Gateacre Tudor style details are already in evidence. These houses are all Grade II listed.

The village has a wide variety of house types of which **Nos. 38** to **42 Gateacre Brow** are good examples of more modest accommodation. Dating back to the late Georgian period, they are of brick construction with typical round arched doorways and small paned windows. They were the affordable housing of their day.

The **Gateacre Unitarian Chapel** was built in 1700 (enlarged in 1719) and is one of the oldest churches in Liverpool. It sits, with its small graveyard, in a prominent position at the heart of the village. Built of local red sandstone with tall arched windows, its most identifiable feature is the small bell tower on the slated roof.

The **Chapel Hall** bears a strong resemblance to the Chapel itself and, although relatively hidden in the centre of the village, its copula on the skyline is a clue to its location. It is entered from Sandfield Road.

No. 28 Gateacre Brow. Built in 1889 for the National Telephone Company to house a local telephone exchange, it was designed by Aubrey Thomas, Architect of the Liver Building. In 1911, the company was taken over by the GPO and it was in use for this purpose until 1946, when it was replaced by an automatic telephone exchange. From 1910, it also accommodated a branch of Parr's Bank which, in 1920, was absorbed into the Westminster Bank, remaining as such until post-World War II, when it was replaced by the Prudential Assurance Company and it now remains mainly in office use. The building has a red sandstone ground floor with its timber and plaster storey supported on brackets in the manner of Tudor buildings. An octagonal turret with a bell-shaped roof is a feature of the corner, and the walls are decorated with three-dimensional plaster panels depicting stories from the Bible. This building, like others of the era, demonstrates clearly the prevailing attitude of the time that public buildings should set an example in quality of both design and materials – a pride that is so lacking in their present-day successors! No. 28 is Grade II listed.

The **Brown Cow** public house on Halewood
Road is a late Victorian Tudor style public house,
with a gabled porch and iron hanging inn sign. It
is Grade II listed and can be said to be a smaller
version of the nearby Black Bull public house.

Around the Village Green

The landscaped triangle of land at the junction of Grange Lane and Gateacre Brow acts as the 'village green' and can be said to be the village centre. Situated in this triangle are the **Wilson Memorial Fountain 1883**, and the **Jubilee Memorial 1887**.

The **Jubilee Memorial 1887** is a red granite column supporting a bronze sculpture of Queen Victoria inscribed by the sculptor, Gleichen. A bronze plaque, to the rear, contains the following inscription:

Presented by Sir Andrew Barclay Walker, High Sheriff of Lancashire 1886-7. Queen Victoria, Queen of Great Britain and Empress of India.

The **Wilson Memorial Fountain 1883** takes the form of a stone open-sided octagonal building with a pyramid roof enclosing a drinking fountain. It is inscribed: *Erected by the people of Gateacre in memory of John Wilson, 1883.* James H. Wilson was Chairman of the Liverpool Water Authority and had the vision to ensure that the city would have a reliable water supply by building reservoirs in North Wales. He lived in what is now Lea Park Golf Club.

The **Memorial** is notable for its unique collection of sculpted panels depicting a variety of fierce looking dragons, salamanders, and an animal-shaped gargoyle. In contrast, two mermaid cherubs playing musical instruments add a touch of humour. The sculpted keystone is in the form of a plaque with a Liver Bird. It predated those on the Liver Building by some 25 years!

To the rear of the memorial is the **Black Bull** public house, a half-timbered, neo-Tudor building with highly decorative windows and a cobbled forecourt, all of which add to the setting of the building. With its dramatic position in the heart of the village and its unique architectural form, the Black Bull has become the instantly recognisable 'emblem' for Gateacre.

Detail of sculpted decorative panels and shield. The cymbal-playing water baby is in direct contrast to the fierce-looking monsters that flank it.

Built originally as a brewery, the **Clegg's Factory** is a good example of a picturesque factory building that would be associated with a Victorian village. It is brick built with decorative panels in red, blue and yellow brick. The roof is of fish scale-shaped slate with a prominent louvre topped with ornate iron cresting and a weather vane. Clegg's were flock manufacturers and like many other cottage industries, have now ceased production. It may, with ingenuity, be suitable for conversion to residential use.

New buildings in conservation areas need not be eyesores. The **Medical Centre** on Gateacre Brow (originally built as a branch of the Midland Bank) is a good example of a modern design that is in sympathy with its surroundings, reflecting the proportions, materials and colouring of the traditional buildings. It is a pity that recent infill buildings are only notable for their banality!

The **Church of St Stephen** was built in 1872-74 by Cornelious Sherlock, architect of the Picton Reading Room. Built of sandstone in the decorated Gothic style, its tall octagonal tower is a prominent landmark which is well placed on Belle Vale Road. Of note, also, is the stained glass by William Morris and Co. Housing, much of which was slum clearance overspill from the inner area of the city, now surrounds the church. When first built, the church would have been located in a rural setting and it is easy to visualise it as a prominent landmark in the surrounding countryside.

Around St Stephen's Church is a group of late nineteenth brick and half-timbered cottages known as **Church Cottages.** Their tall, clustered, diagonally-set chimneys are a distinctive feature. The above block fronts Belle Vale Road and the others are set at right angles from the road.

Saurer Cottages form a group with **Paradise Cottages** and they were built in 1896. The buildings, in Tudor style, enclose an open courtyard at the front and, as is often the case in the village, they conform in scale and proportion to their neighbours. Brick has been chosen as the means of construction with small, panelled stone-mullioned windows.

Nos. 6 and **9 Belle Vale Road** are part of a group of houses dating back to the first part of the nineteenth century. Built of sandstone ashlar blocks with slate roofs, they provide yet another example of how individual identity can be achieved within a discipline of good proportion and respect for community identity.

These Grange Lane buildings are listed Grade II.

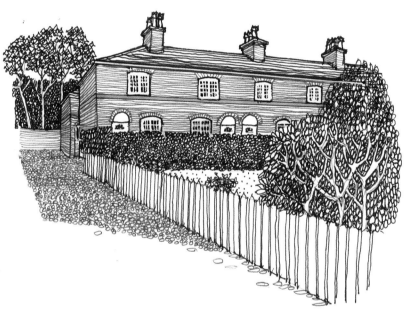

Paradise Cottages in Grange Lane probably date from the early eighteenth century and are built of rough sandstone with ashlar lintels over the windows and boarded and studded doors. Much alteration and addition has taken place in recent years but the original design can still be appreciated, in spite of the later embellishments.

Set back from Grange Lane are two parallel rows of small cottages known as **York Cottages**. Built of brick in the early nineteenth century, these fine cottages have round arched doorways, blind fanlights and sliding sash windows.

When Trams Came to Woolton

The year is 1949 and a tram stands in the Woolton terminus ready to take passengers into town. The gable of the building, now Kitchencene, is much as it is today and the Salisbury farm building (though not painted white) is readily identifiable. A stone-built building occupies the site of the present post office – surely the most inappropriate new building ever to be placed in a conservation area. Buffers, used here as seats, were designed to prevent the trams from escaping down Kings Drive. Belisha pedestrian poles at the crossing hark back to the days when pedestrians were given priority over vehicles. The terminus area is now a car park.

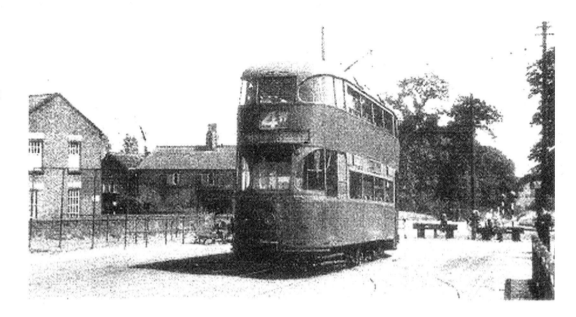

A tram emerges from the central reservation on High Street to turn into Menlove Avenue on its journey into town. Much of the route was on dedicated carriageways – a design perfected in the outer city by the visionary City Engineer, James Brodie. The terraced houses on High Street were much as they are today but note the car parked facing in the direction of Menlove Avenue – in those days traffic was two way on both High Streets! Note also the pram being pushed across the pedestrian crossing at Menlove Avenue. Not many would have the courage to do that today!